the little book of
SPIRITUALISM

Published by OH!
20 Mortimer Street
London W1T 3JW

Disclaimer:
This book and the information contained herein are for general educational and entertainment use only. The contents are not claimed to be exhaustive, and the book is sold on the understanding that neither the publishers nor the author are thereby engaged in rendering any kind of professional services. Users are encouraged to confirm the information contained herein with other sources and review the information carefully with their appropriate, qualified service providers. Neither the publishers nor the author shall have any responsibility to any person or entity regarding any loss or damage whatsoever, direct or indirect, consequential, special or exemplary, caused or alleged to be caused, by the use or misuse of information contained in this book.

ISBN 978-1-91161-086-1

Editorial consultant: Sasha Fenton
Editorial: Victoria Godden
Project manager: Russell Porter
Design: Ben Ruocco
Production: Freencky Portas

A CIP catalogue record for this book is available from the British Library

Printed in China

10 9 8 7 6 5 4 3 2 1

the little book of
SPIRITUALISM

tracie long

CONTENTS

INTRODUCTION

THIS LITTLE BOOK WILL BE YOUR SPIRITUAL GUIDE,

there to comfort and inspire you on good days and bad. Just know that whenever you are feeling a little helpless, lost or alone, this book will bring you encouragement and the hope that things will get better.

In it, I share the techniques, thoughts, quotes and affirmations that Spirit has shown me in my spiritual journey, and give you the assurance that you always have someone supporting you and guiding you.

If you picked up this book because it sparked your interest, maybe it's time for you to learn how to understand those little nudges that you have had. You will also learn from the past, because it is the past that makes you who you are today, so that you can move forward in your unique journey towards enlightenment.

It's a beautiful thing to find inner peace and share what you have learnt along the way in your search for information, while you help and inspire others. We are all here to learn, love, help and be kind to each other. I hope you feel uplifted and inclined to learn more as you work your way through this book.

CHAPTER

1

SPIRITUALISM

Spiritualism can mean many things to many people.

To some, it is a religion; to most, it provides evidence that there is life after death; and to others, it is the life-long study to gain enlightenment, peace and spiritual wisdom.

Whatever Spiritualism may mean, it is a journey that involves finding one's spirituality to bring about some sort of transformation.

It also enhances our spiritual qualities, morals and ethics, ultimately letting us become better versions of ourselves.

the SPIRIT WORLD

As some of you may already know, a medium can communicate with those in the spirit world. They are often born with this ability. The primary purpose of communicating with the spirit world is to provide the evidence that there is life after death, for those of you who go for readings, sittings or who visit the spiritualist churches and centres.

You might be wondering what Spirit is. To put it simply, Spirit is a form of energy that cannot be destroyed; it can only change its form.

When a person dies, the physical body is left behind while the soul continues to exist in a different dimension called the spirit world.

Those who already believe in Spiritualism know that as we move through life, we make choices, and the outcome of those choices affects our soul's growth. Then, when we leave this earthly life, we may look back over the life we lived, and then have the opportunity to take stock and decide what we might have done differently, and consider what we must do next time when we choose to return.

the SIGNS of SPIRITUAL AWAKENING

There are some common signs that you are awakening spiritually. While you may only experience a few of these, some people can encounter all of them.

You might notice that you have increased empathy and intuition; you may find yourself listening less to what people say and paying more attention to the feeling you get by being around them, while also tuning in to the intention behind their words or actions.

You might want to be out in nature more often, and at times you may get distracted when walking outside, just looking at flowers, birds or the sky.

You may not want to be around negative people or behaviours, and you might find that you are less interested in gossip, pettiness, other people's moans or their judgement of others. You could experience a strong desire to be around like-minded people, and you often feel drained by arguments, unpleasant energies or the news on the television.

You may become upset by images of a negative nature and tend to feel the emotions of people around you. So, if others are sad or negative, you will feel that way. Feeling and believing that all life is sacred, you could find yourself taking small insects outside rather than squashing them. You may start to think about the welfare of animals, and you may feel drawn to becoming a vegan or vegetarian.

Your consciousness may feel renewed, and when you look back on your own life experience, you might realize that your life can be different based on the awareness you have now developed. You may start to live more "in the moment", becoming less interested in asking yourself the "what if" questions about the future or looking back to the past.

You may find a sense of inner peace, preferring to have a quiet time or spending time alone. You may find you tend to turn off the television, especially the news and social media, and read self-help or inspiring stories and books on positivity.

You may notice that you are more compassionate and positive, rather than feeling ill will towards others. You wish them well and hope they will find happiness because, in reality, you realize we all are connected. You may need less attention when you're around your friends and family, and you would rather watch, assist and help others when you can.

CHAPTER

2

the DIFFERENCE BETWEEN a PSYCHIC and a MEDIUM

The arguments about what mediums, psychics and, indeed, clairvoyants are have raged for decades.

Everyone has different ideas, partly because the wrong titles are often given to the wrong skills, so confusion reigns.

As you go through this book, you will discover what these people do and also what other sensitive people can do with their gifts.

While learning all this, you will find out what your own skills are and how to develop them.

A MEDIUM

A medium can prove that life exists after death. They do this by contacting loved ones that have died and passing on messages from them to the seeker. The seeker should be able to understand the message or the characteristics of the person who has passed on, as given by the medium, and this must be information that the medium could not possibly know about the deceased.

Mediums can lift their energy so they vibrate on a higher frequency, while Spirit can lower theirs slightly so they can meet in the middle, at which point Spirit and the medium can communicate.

This is where the term *medium* may come from, as it means being a channel for information.

A PSYCHIC

A psychic will give you some insight or guidance about what is happening with situations in your life, especially if you are feeling stuck or unsure about something. Some psychics can predict an outcome or see what the future will hold over the coming months and, in some cases, years.

Many psychics use tarot cards or other tools as well as their spirit guides, angels or spirit helpers to tune in and give guidance.

The advice given is open to change, depending on the decisions that the seeker makes. The future is not set in stone, and some psychics will provide options and outcomes to help the questioner decide which path to take or decision to make. The choice, however, is really up to the questioner.

CHOOSING a MEDIUM or PSYCHIC

When looking for a medium or a psychic for a reading, try to go by recommendation.

Ask around, because someone you know will be bound to have seen one or know someone that has.

Check them out, see how long they have been working as a medium or psychic, take a look at their website or profile and read their feedback before you make a booking or part with any money.

TERMINOLOGY

The terms used for psychics or mediums may be a little confusing, so here are some of the typical definitions:

psychic medium: a medium
who is also a psychic

mental medium: a medium
who perceives the Spirit through
the mind, using the skills of
clairvoyance (clear seeing),
clairsentience (clear sensing)
and/or clairaudience (clear
hearing)

physical medium: a medium
who can manifest ectoplasm so that
you can see the outline of a spirit
person (rare nowadays)

transfiguration medium:
a medium whose face will become
covered in a spiritual veil, upon
which the faces of people in Spirit
will appear

direct voice medium:
a medium who can manifest
distinctive voices and accents

trance medium: a medium
who allows the spirits to speak
directly through him or her (also
called channelling)

spiritual medium: a medium
who is also a spiritualist

BECOMING a MEDIUM

To become a practising medium within Spiritualism is not easy. Psychic mediums must know a lot about diverse topics and complete several courses and other forms of training. More importantly, they must be able to demonstrate and give evidence in front of a group of people who also know the subject.

"When the impossible
has been eliminated,
all that remains no
matter how improbable
is possible."

ARTHUR CONAN DOYLE

CHAPTER

3

we all have
SPIRIT
GUIDES

We are all blessed with spirit guides who surround us and support us, and we usually have more than one. I have four; they are all males, and they each step forward depending on what I'm doing at the time.

Our leading spirit guide is with us from birth, and the rest of the guides tend to join us or make themselves known to us as we progress on our journey through life. Their help can be both practical and spiritual in nature.

Most of us forget who we were before we reincarnated, where we have come from and the life we lived before.

We also forget our purpose this time around. Spirit guides know that it is challenging to be incarnated here on earth while keeping a connection to your higher self and continuing your soul's purpose.

the ROLE of YOUR GUIDES

The role of your guides is to lead you gently but consistently by intuitive nudges to stay on track with your soul's purpose.

If you need to accomplish something to achieve your mission in this lifetime, you will find support and help from your spirit guides.

They will link you to resources,
people and, in some cases, the
money you need. They will lead you
to books to help you reach your
goals, and they will offer insight and
comfort when you feel lost.

Your spirit guides will help you
accomplish and achieve things that
honour the purpose that you set for
yourself before you incarnated.

I know that it is probably not in my soul's purpose to win the lottery, because I don't have to carry out something in this life that requires that kind of money. Instead, I know that I can receive help from the continued growth that I experience and the studying I do, and by using my gifts to tap in to abundance.

So, if I were to ask my spirit guides to help me win the lottery, I'm sure they wouldn't oblige.

HOW YOUR GUIDES can HELP YOU

You don't need highly developed
abilities to begin getting to know
and working with your spirit guides,
because while you may not be able
to see them, your guides can certainly
see you.

You only need to set an intention, and
they will notice it, or you can speak
to them aloud, and they will hear you.
I often do this, and now I trust that I
will be given what I have asked for if it
serves my higher purpose.

One way of setting your guides to work is to request their help with specific goals.

You can get into the habit of doing this by writing down your goals, say for the coming week and month, and then asking your guides for help in achieving each of them.

for example:

- I would like X amount of money each month to pay my rent.

- I would like to work with X number of clients next month to meet my outgoings.

- I'd like to spend X more hours per week of quality time with my friends and family.

- I'd like more fun and laughter in my life.

Your guides will not intervene until you ask them, because to do so would go against your free will, but asking for their help is powerful, and they like to have something to do.

By not asking, you are making them redundant when they want to help you. Once you do ask, you won't look back, other than to question why you didn't do it before.

If you are unsure how to start, try saying the following aloud:

*"To my spirit guides,
I request your help in achieving
my goals, and hopefully these
goals are aligned with my
highest purpose.
Please help me to recognize
your assistance and
the opportunities when they
manifest. Thank you."*

Your spirit guides work to help you manifest your desires, often in the most unexpected ways.

I realized a long time ago that I have a specific, leading guide, and he connects me with the clients who would benefit from a session with me. He also gives me the heads-up when I have a client who is about to contact me.

Be open-minded and the universe will send you the resources you need in all sorts of creative ways.

If you only expect to receive help through one specific channel, you may miss or discard the support that shows up in other ways.

Going back to the list on page 49, if you requested financial assistance, you may receive a gift of money to help with bills.

If you wanted more fun, you might get invited to a party or meet a new friend who makes you laugh and with whom you want to spend more time, and they may know a lot of people who are looking for what you have to offer.

You may come across a book or find something that sparks your interest on the internet, leading you where you need to be.

There are many possibilities, so you must be open to them all by seeing the opportunity in every experience that comes your way.

Some of you may have religious backgrounds and have been taught that to invoke the spiritual side of life means you need to pray, to ask very politely or even to plead, but you do not have to do this.

Your guides can see the bigger picture. They are your helpers in Spirit, and there really is no need to barter with them or to ask for what you want over and over again, because while this may amuse your guides, it won't get them to work any faster for you.

"*Matter is spirit
at its lowest level.
Spirit is matter at
its highest level.*"

H. P. BLAVATSKY

GETTING TO KNOW
HOW SPIRIT GUIDES WORK

If you are visual, your spirit guide
may pop into your mind's eye with
a message on a board, or they may
show you an image that means
something to you.

If you're clairaudient, you may become
aware of an inner voice speaking to
you, or words from songs that appear
in your head that hold a message.

Over the years, I have developed all my senses to be able to work with Spirit, so my guides work with me in a variety of ways. I'm also very clairsentient, and my guides connect with me by giving me a tingling sensation on the side of my head, usually around my left ear. When this happens, I know I need to be aware or to listen carefully, because a message is coming.

MEETING YOUR SPIRIT GUIDES

One of the primary reasons for discovering who is guiding you is to obtain information that's not available to your normal level of consciousness. Your guide becomes your "go-to" person when you need answers or guidance.

There are some things that you are not meant to know and others that you are expected to experience. However, your guides are excellent helpers in emergencies and for spiritual development.

Spirit guides are entities that watch, teach, heal and help you on your physical journey into higher consciousness. Communication is telepathic. It comes through clairaudience and clairvoyance during meditation, dreams or just learning how to focus your thoughts and quieten your mind so that you can receive messages.

Some people call this channelling. The more you practise, the easier it gets. Each of your guides comes to you for a specific purpose, like healing, receiving messages or spiritual development.

If you think the time is right for you to meet one of your spirit guides, find a quiet place that is free of distractions, relax and get comfortable. Clear your mind and focus on your guide.

You may sense the presence of your spirit guide, or you may feel physical sensations on your body, such as pressure on the top of your head or the opening of the crown chakra.

In case you are not yet familiar with
the chakras and their functions, there
are seven main chakras with which
we work. They make up the energy
system connecting the spine and
the various organs that run through
your body.

You might want to do some research
on chakras, as they make a fascinating
subject.

Sometimes you will feel a sensation on the left side of the body or face; some people feel a little heat and others feel a slight cool breeze. It is generally the left, as the left side receives information, while the right side sends it out.

The left side goes to the right side of the brain, which is the intuitive side.

You may want to ask your guide for a name or to see what they look like, because by doing this, you will feel more connected to them.

If you have trouble hearing the name or deciphering messages, write down what you think you are being given, as you might find that more manageable.

CHAPTER

4

MEETING your GUIDES

In this chapter I will
show you how to put
yourself into the frame of
mind that will help you
reach your guides.

I will also give you some meditation techniques that will open you up to Spirit. If it doesn't work the first time, leave it for a day or two and then try again. It may be that you weren't in the right frame of mind the first time around. The next thing you will now learn is to open up to Spirit while protecting yourself from unwanted psychic intrusion.

MAKING
a START

These steps work together
to help you establish a
relationship with your spirit
guides!

step 1

- Sit quietly and pay attention to your breathing.

- Imagine that you are inside a giant bubble of white light that surrounds you, just like a big dome. This closed dome is a protective energy field around your physical and spiritual body, and it allows you to be safe and comfortable.

step 2

- Tell your spirit guides that you are ready to open up and understand any information they may have for you.

- Now imagine that this big dome opens.

- As it does so, you become more aware of your ability to see and hear psychically.

step 3

- You are now able to communicate with your spirit guides and feel their energy.

- Pay close attention to the sensations that you feel, see and hear.

step 4

- Once you get comfortable doing this, you can also ask your guides to help with information that other spirits want to tell you, such as hearing from relatives that have passed away.

step 5

- Ask your guides to allow only positive and uplifting information to be sent to you. They can do this because your spirit guides are with you to help you, and they can be your mediators with other spirit people.

CLOSING DOWN

When you feel you have finished talking with your guides, visualize closing the big dome of white light around you again. You will know when you have done this correctly because you will be totally shut off from the energies and spirits.

You may even recite a special saying such as: "I'm closing down now," or: "Can you please make sure that I have my protection back in place."

Thank your guides for helping,
for connecting with you and for
protecting you. Then get up and walk
around, drink some water or eat
something light.

After doing this whole process several
times, you will start to recognize what
it feels like to open and close your
energy field.

When you start doing this, I recommend writing in a journal and keeping a record of your experiences and of any messages you receive, because these messages often slip away from your memory. However, it's useful to review them at a later date.

Sometimes things don't always make sense, but they may well do later, and this will also help you to interpret your messages.

Closing down properly after doing any form of spiritual work is even more important than opening up in the first place.

When I'm not working, I try to keep myself closed down, because if I opened up to all the energies or vibrations around me, I would be a worn-out wreck. I can tell when I'm not closed down properly, as I start to feel drained.

MEDITATION

Meditation can help you connect to your guides, but it can also help you to increase your happiness and improve your focus, memory, compassion and productivity, as well as teaching you how to be present in the moment. It can raise your awareness, decrease stress levels, reduce anxiety, increase your capacity for optimism, improve your health and give you inner peace.

You might have heard the saying: *"You cannot pour from an empty cup."*

Self-care is a particularly important part of your spiritual journey, but what does self-care mean? It can mean learning about different techniques and meditations to find out what your requirements are and what works best for you.

We all need time to nourish ourselves and to discover which different practices are available and which will leave us feeling supported, uplifted and refreshed.

MEDITATION
to MEET your
SPIRIT GUIDES

This meditation and
visualization will help you
encounter your own spirit
guides.

This meditation came to me from my primary spirit guide, and I have used it many times in my development circles (see page 139). If you would like to try it, you may want to read through it a few times so you can visualize it.

However, an even better option is to record it on your phone so you can play it back to yourself while you are doing the meditation. When you have finished, remember to record your experiences in your journal for future reference.

- Visualize yourself walking along a path.

- This path will look just the way you would like it to look.

- As you bring the path into focus in your mind's eye, you will see a lush green forest in the distance.

- Now visualize yourself walking along this path and, as you do, notice the silence and the peacefulness when you wander among the trees.

- Notice how the gentle breeze causes the leaves of trees and plants to sway and dance.

- You can hear your own footsteps as you enjoy the pleasant walk, fully immersing yourself in your senses.

- After some time, you hear the distant sound of flowing water, somewhere beyond the trees.

- As you walk further along the path, you come across a spacious clearing.

- The sun is shining down into the clearing and illuminating a stone bridge ahead of you.

- Below the bridge, you see water; it's calm, and a shallow river runs from right to left.

- The sun shimmers off the surface of the clear blue water.

- The bridge itself is broad, so you have plenty of room to cross.

- At the other end of the bridge, you see some steps that lead up to a stone archway, wholly covered in beautiful green vines and leaves.

- At each side of the archway is a stone wall also covered in beautiful green vines and leaves that seem to grow in both directions.

- Whatever is beyond the archway is not yet known to you, for you cannot see over the stone walls.

- Now visualize yourself walking across the stone bridge towards the archway.

- As you walk, you feel distinct sensations of peace and love coming to you.

- With each step, you feel your old physical life fade further and further away as if it were a distant memory.

- You feel you have come a long way, yet time has no meaning here, and it does not concern you.

- As you cross the bridge and approach the steps directly in front of the archway, you become aware that the view beyond the arch is somehow distorted.

- You feel a sense of beckoning love and familiar belonging ahead.

- As you step through the arch, suddenly all your surroundings change.

- You immediately sense penetrating warmth that engulfs you like a loving blanket.

- You find yourself upon a wide path, completely covered in flower petals of all colours.

- At each side of the trail, there appears to be a long hedge, made from hundreds and hundreds of different flowers of all description.

- It is the most beautiful display of colour and nature you have ever seen.

- There is also a magical fragrance that captivates your very soul.

- The flowers seem to come alive with your presence.

- The two hedges direct you down the path and, as you follow it, you begin to make out a structure ahead.

- You immediately recognize it,
  for it is your dream cottage – your
  soul sanctuary, your sacred home
  away from home, and your special
  secret place.

- You are very excited to see it here,
  and you waste no time going inside.

- Once inside, you can visualize your
  surroundings just as you want them
  to be.

- You find everything you value here –
  everything you have ever had or ever
  wanted.

- The architecture is as you wish – as are the pictures, ornaments and all the furnishings.

- You make your way into the main room, since you are expecting your guest any time now, and prepare the place as you wish, ready for your spirit guide's arrival.

- You take a seat in front of a beautiful fireplace.

- This is your sacred cottage; nobody may enter without your permission, and you are entirely safe and at peace here.

- Today you have invited one of your spirit guides, and while you wait you ponder the questions you may wish to ask him.

- And now is the time – silently and gracefully your spirit guide enters the room.

- He appears to you in a form that you can relate to, and feel comfortable with.

- His presence radiates complete unconditional love, compassion and wisdom.

- Your spirit guide speaks first, introducing his name and telling you who he is.

- He holds a gift for you, which he places in your hands.

- This gift can be anything, but it will be personal and significant to you.

- Greet him, thank him for this gift and invite him to sit with you.

- This is your opportunity to ask any questions you may have.

- Spend as much time as you need, and exchange all that you feel you need to.

- When you have finished your conversation, thank him for coming and for his advice and comfort.

- He will leave the room as silently and gracefully as he entered it.

- You will be left feeling spiritually empowered, and full of joy and gratitude.

- When you are ready to leave, remember to take your gift with you, make your way out of your cottage and back along the path of flowers. Go through the archway, back over the bridge, and follow your way back along the path into the lush green forest.

- Allow yourself to become aware of your physical body within the physical world.

- Bring your focus back and concentrate on your breathing when you are ready to open your eyes.

CHAPTER

5

the ANGELIC REALM

Whatever stage of your spiritual
path you have reached, you
will more than likely have heard
about angels. Angels can help
and guide you every step of the
way if you allow them to do so.

The more you open up to the
guidance and love of the angels,
the more your life will improve.
Your life can become more
relaxed when working with the
angels, because all you need
to do is to ask and be open to
their help.

CALLING upon
your ANGELS

Learn how to communicate with
your angels and guardian angels,
and receive messages about any
questions you have.

If you are just starting out on your spiritual journey, then working with the angelic realm is often the right choice. It seems a lot less daunting than the spirit world does, and many people find calling upon angels a great comfort.

The following steps indicate that you are ready to meet your angels.

- You have become interested in some spiritual matters, and you are exploring further, using books, courses and other training methods.

- You have reached a point where you feel there is more to life than materialism, and you are no longer satisfied with your old way of life.

- You feel as if you are being called upon to do something more with your life.

- You have already begun developing a new path; you have started training or studying, and you may now want a new career, like offering healing, readings or treatments.

- You have been on your new path for a while, and you can now see the bigger picture of why you are here. You are finding your purpose, and you are busy following it with a happy heart.

WHAT are ANGELS?

Angels are higher beings of light who, when asked, respond to us by giving guidance, assistance, protection and comfort. Our angels are here to help us, especially when we set the intention to bring joy and healing to ourselves and others. You can ask for angels to surround your loved ones, your home and your business, because they love to help.

You may have also heard of
archangels, which are the angels who
supervise the guardian angels and the
lesser angels. You can also call upon an
archangel whenever you need help.

Angels and archangels cannot intervene unless we ask them to help, and it is up to us to connect with them and to invite them into our lives.

The only exception to this is if we encounter a life-threatening situation where we could be in danger of death before it is our time.

ANGEL CARDS

If you are unsure where to start, you could buy yourself a pack of angel cards, which are great for receiving guidance.

Just choose a pack that you are drawn to, and then take the time to get to know them. When you are ready to use them, remember to put yourself into the right mindset.

First, ask your angels to ground and protect you before requesting their guidance and the answers to any questions you may have.

Pick up the cards, read the messages on them and those in the booklet that comes with the cards, and then allow your intuition to guide you.

TYPES of ANGELS

We are all born with a guardian angel, and they are with us every time our souls reincarnate. We also have a "kindle angel".

I call mine "my little helper angel", and I call upon this one for help with lesser matters.

I am sure that some of you may have heard of the parking angel.

When I need a parking space or a particular spot, I just ask my parking angel to help, and, most of the time, I find just what I want nearby. I also ask this one to help me have safe and stress-free journeys.

I also call upon the angels for important tasks like helping spirits that are grounded. This will take a little explanation. When someone is near death, an angel will come to take him over to the other side.

However, some spirits decide not to go over when the time comes, and then they discover that they need help because they are stuck in the wrong place.

Those of us who work with Spirit can communicate with the spiritual realm and talk with angels, and we can help the angels to take the stuck person over to where they need to be. This is sometimes called "rescue mediumship", because we rescue the soul and guide it to the other side.

I call upon angels when I need divine guidance, but I can tell you that it took some time before I could tell the difference in the energy that I receive from spiritual guides or from angels.

I was lucky enough to see an angel, and it's a magical experience that I will never forget. It feels like an honour, and it was the most fantastic experience.

Since that day, I have no doubts about their existence, and I have been grateful for the help they have given me over the years.

Many angels help us and the planet; there are too many to list. However, if you do some research, you will come across many names, some of which are familiar, such as the archangels Michael and Gabriel.

However, there are many names that you will not have heard of – or perhaps even be able to pronounce!

"All things that ever were,
that are, or that will be,
having; their record upon the
astral light, or tablet of the unseen
universe, the initiated adept,
by using the vision of his own
spirit, can know all that has been
known or can be known."

H. P. BLAVATSKY

the RANKS
of the ANGELS

In total, there are nine levels of angels. This is a summary and hierarchy of the angels, from highest to lowest.

SERAPHIM

Seraphim are the highest order of the hierarchy of angels. These angelic beings spend their time worshipping and praising God.

CHERUBIM

Cherubim are the second highest order, and they are depicted on the Ark of the Covenant as its guardians. God sent these angels to guard Eden after the expulsion of Adam and Eve.

THRONES

Thrones are the third-ranking order of angels. These angels were often believed to be deployed like charioteers around the Throne of God.

DOMINIONS

Dominions are the fourth-ranking order of angels. These angels decide the success or failure of nations. Dominions have been described as wearing long *albs*, which are gowns that reach down to their feet.

VIRTUES

Virtues are the fifth-ranking order of angels. They have been called "The Brilliant or Shining Ones", as well as the angels of miracles, encouragement and blessings. They are said to be involved with people who are struggling with their faith.

POWERS

Powers are the sixth-ranking order of angels. They are responsible for maintaining the border between Heaven and Earth. It is also believed that, at death, the Powers are the ones that guide our transition to Heaven.

PRINCIPALITIES

Principalities are the seventh-ranking order of angels. These angels act as the guardians over the nations and the leaders of the world. They are given the task of managing the duties of the angels. Principalities have been described as dressed in soldiers' uniforms with golden girdles.

ARCHANGELS

Archangels are the eighth-ranking order of angels. You may be more familiar with these. Archangel Michael is believed to be the highest-ranking warrior angel in God's heavenly host, while Archangel Gabriel is the highest-ranking messenger angel, and the one who brings special tidings to God's people.

GUARDIAN ANGELS

Guardian angels are the last order of angels. In some cases, the guardian angel serves only as a messenger, but in others, the angel lingers in visible form, taking responsibility for the wellbeing of individuals in trouble, guarding them from harm and leading them out of danger.

CHAPTER

6

ASSOCIATED METHODS and IDEAS

One idea linked to Spiritualism is reincarnation, a subject in which many spiritual people hold strong beliefs.

Why do we choose to reincarnate? Why would we want to come back again?

Well, to put it simply, it is part of the soul's journey to return more than once and to complete the lessons we set for our soul's growth until it reaches enlightenment.

By looking into your past lives, you can discover the experiences for which you came back to earth.

You can find out what sex you were before, where you lived and who you were with. You can learn whether the relationship you have in your current lifetime was also part of a past life.

However, confusingly, the relationship may have changed. For instance, you may be a parent to the other person now, but you may have been his or her child last time round.

TRY MEDITATION

Meditation is an effective way to delve into your past lives, especially if you feel that you have been here before.

This is particularly the case if you experience feelings of "déjà vu". This is where you get a sense that you have visited a place before, or when you meet a new person with whom you instantly feel connected.

Often, we are reincarnated with our family, partners and friends, and sometimes with those to whom we feel drawn. Going into past lives can be useful if you have phobias, unexplained illnesses or situations that keep recurring.

I have done this many times through my shamanic healing sessions. I have found the underlying cause of something, such as helping someone to heal a phobia, or uncovered something half-remembered. This can reveal the story behind something that is locked deep within the person's subconscious.

TOOLS

There are many tools that you can use that will enhance your spiritual journey. These may be crystals (see page 141), tarot and oracle cards, psychometry, crystal balls, pendulums, dowsing, auras and chakras.

DEVELOPMENT CIRCLES

It's a great idea to attend a development circle. This is a group of like-minded people who come together in a safe environment to explore various methods, to enhance their spiritual knowledge and to practise their art. A *closed* circle is a bit like a club, as only those who have been invited can join. In a closed circle, you are more likely to try the different mediumship techniques.

Do some research and make sure the group or teacher you pick has good intentions and a good reputation. Check that they have some form of teaching qualification or experience in the field of Spiritualism. If you cannot find a circle in your area, I suggest that you read as many books as you can, look online and maybe take some online courses or attend workshops.

CRYSTALS

Among the things I love are crystals, and I think that they are an excellent subject to study. Crystals have a long tradition of being used for healing. Each crystal has a unique internal structure that causes it to resonate at a specific frequency, and this is said to give crystals their healing properties. They can help to restore stability and balance to the body's energy systems, therefore stimulating the body's natural healing mechanisms.

They are also useful for grounding, opening up and protection.

I have many crystals around my house, and I also wear them as jewellery. I use crystals for my shamanic healing sessions and, of course, for grounding and protection.

"The physical basis of all psychic belief is that the soul is a complete duplicate of the body, resembling it in the smallest particular, although constructed in some far more tenuous material. In ordinary conditions these two bodies are intermingled so that the identity of the finer one is entirely obscured. At death, however, and under certain conditions in the course of life, the two divide and can be seen separately."

ARTHUR CONAN DOYLE, "The Vital Message", 1919

CHAPTER

7

AFFIRMATIONS

Affirmations have a long history, with many appearing in the Bible. The ones in this chapter are a modern take on the same idea. So let these simple sayings give you comfort, reassurance and advice when you most need it most. They are sourced from my own spiritual guides and several other people in the world of Spiritualism.

modern
AFFIRMATIONS

"You can expect wonderful blessings of all kinds to enter your life, and these blessings are to be shared with your close friends and loved ones; put them to good use. You are supported and loved by your family in Spirit. Trust in the healing process. It's now time to honour your feelings, so surround yourself with care and invest the love you give to others on yourself."

"Happiness comes from within;
it is not dependant on other
people, and you become sad
and lose your power when your
happiness depends on the actions
of other people. Spend time alone,
or in nature, to reflect and be
still. It's okay to cherish and love
yourself; never give your power
away to others."

"We see you, we hear you, nothing goes unnoticed, and we see the inner work you have been doing. We walk beside you, guiding you to your soul purpose and showing you signs which will lead you to achieve your highest good. Be open to receiving our messages, nothing is ever by chance."

"I wish you could see what I see;
the incredible potential within
you that would allow you to
accomplish wonderful things. Shine
your light, be brave and surround
yourself with inspiring, like-minded
people who work on a high
vibration. They will lift your Spirit.
If you ever feel alone or stumble,
remember that I walk beside you
always. I am your guide. I am your
guardian angel."

"Keep your heart singing, keep your mind clear, keep facing forward towards the light, stay positive and find joy. It's the best medicine. Look up, smile at rainbows and leave the past and the shadows behind you."

"Your body is made up of the physical, the mental and the spiritual. Each has its own vibrations, which must work together to make a whole. You must make each a priority to find inner peace, health and happiness on this journey through life."

AFFIRMATIONS
for those who have
SUFFERED
TRAUMA

"It could be that you are not healing because you are trying to be who you were before the trauma, but that person doesn't exist anymore. There is a new person just waiting to be set free. Bring some passion and life into that person, and then see how things begin to change."

"You are seeking a new path of personal and spiritual discovery and, yes, it is likely to be an intense spiritual path, so you may choose to keep this journey private at this time. You also know that inspiration and understanding come from within and from self-study, rather than looking to others for answers."

CHAPTER

8

YOUR
SPIRITUAL
JOURNEY

You are in the middle of
the inner journey, and the
shift you are feeling is taking
you away from a place
of emotional turmoil, grief
and loss.

It may be scary and painful at times, but you will get through it; so just take it one day at a time. You are closer than you think; the universe is supporting you, so don't waver – just follow the path that feels right and that lights your soul.

We can never plan the way we want things to go, but don't worry, for things will be better than you could possibly imagine. You will be supported no matter what, so trust that you will always be guided.

Take note of your dreams and of any recurring thoughts.

You will soon start to receive
messages that your guides love you
and that they are with you in Spirit,
so walk steady, walk tall and be brave,
because they will walk beside you.

BOUNDARIES

Did you know that having clear
boundaries is a spiritual act?
Spirituality is learning to say *no* and
let others know where you stand,
so only say *yes* to things you can do
with a happy heart. Learn to go with
your instinct and your feelings when
deciding things; otherwise your energy
will become depleted, and you will be
left feeling resentful or used.

GOOD and
BAD TIMES

A life well lived contains loss and tragedy as well as triumph and adventure, so if you are going through a difficult time, rather than cursing and blaming others, try to find the blessing hidden in the situation. The very thing you thought would break you is often a breakthrough.

the SOUL PLAN

If you feel unprepared or worried, know that you came into this world with a soul plan. You have been here many times before, and you are now ready to embrace your gifts and the wisdom that's hidden within you. Step into the light and don't be afraid, because you have been prepared for this.

LINK with YOUR GUIDES

Take time to meditate, to link with your guides, angels and spirits, for they are the keepers of all wisdom, and they will give you the answers you seek. Imagine yourself surrounded by a bright white light and lift your vibration. Do not look outside for guidance; listen to your inner voice.

TAKE CARE of YOURSELF

It's essential to take care of your body, to be aware of how it feels and honour what your soul needs. Rest is important. It isn't being lazy, but being kind to yourself, so sleep when you want to and eat when you want to, so you can continue to share your light with others.

PROSPERITY
is ALLOWED

As you start to follow your heart, prosperity will come to you, and your angels will help you release any negative thoughts or feelings you have about money. You deserve the best, and it will be yours, so you are being urged to keep moving forward, to listen to your instincts and to go with your heart rather than with any negative programming that may be in your head.

EXPECT ENVY

You are flying high and reaching for the stars, so others may feel jealous or threatened by your success, but don't let that put you off. After a time, they will become inspired by your achievements and encouraged to follow your example. You will light the way for others, because you will become a leader.

CHILDREN and ADULTS

You may have a gift for working with young children and adults. If so, it is your divine purpose in this lifetime to help those who are young and sensitive by parenting them or teaching them.

If you are a little confused about where to begin, why not do some research? Your guide will lead you to the right information.

HEALING

Your natural spiritual gifts make you a wonderfully successful healer. Whether you conduct energy work, counselling or some other form of physical or psychological therapy, always remember to bring through the divine healing force.

You don't need to drain your own energy because there is an unlimited supply readily available for you to tap in to.

CLAIRVOYANCE

You may develop clairvoyance, which is the ability to see colours, images and visions with the mind's eye, along with dreams and symbols. These help us to make sense of this world and of the world of Spirit.

You can receive clairvoyant images in the form of psychic flashes, or as personal memories that come into your mind, to help and heal someone who has a situation that needs solving.

a DREAM JOURNAL

If you have very vivid dreams,
keeping a dream journal is a way to
help you and enhance your clairvoyant
abilities. Make sure you have pen and
paper close by so that, when you wake
up, you can record what happened
and the messages you received in
your dreams.

CHANGE
and DEVELOPMENT

You are a sensitive soul, and it is now time to face this fact and make some changes. You will have noticed that your interests and tastes have shifted, and what once interested you no longer appeals to you. You're more sensitive to the energies of the people and the places you visit. You need gentle environments with supportive people around you. You also need a career that you feel good about, and which gives meaning to your life.

TRUST
YOUR INTUITION

Follow your heart and trust your intuition to lead you to the opportunities that align with your highest good. Let your feelings and emotions guide you, so when something feels fantastic, do more of it, and when something doesn't feel right, do less of it. Allow your inner guidance to lead the way. Seek out opportunities that fulfil you and that align with your personal values rather than following the path others expect you to take.

CHANGING VALUES

Notice your natural passions and interests. They are guideposts directing you towards the actions that you can take within your local community that might help you to protect animals and nature. You will develop a special bond with animals, so if you have been thinking of getting a pet or giving a poor stray a home, you will bring them great comfort and healing. Animals are naturally drawn to you, and they can sense your incredible energy.

WHO IS RESPONSIBLE?

When you feel upset about an issue, it may be a sign regarding your purpose, and whenever you think that *someone* should do something about *something*, know that this vague *someone* is probably meant to be you.

EVERYDAY AFFIRMATIONS

- I shall experience abundance in every area of my life.

- I will have money, time, friends and opportunity.

- I will allow the abundance of the universe to flow to me and through me with ease and grace.

- I am grateful for all that I have in my life.

- I am willing to forgive myself for past mistakes.

- I forgive friends and family that may have caused me upset and harm.

- As I forgive, I will let go of all past resentments.

- I am now free to live my life in peace and harmony, filled with joy.

GATHER NEW KNOWLEDGE

Now is the right time to learn new things, to study and gather information, so just enjoy being a student for now, because in the future, you will use the knowledge you have gained. Take action, because you are being given that little push from Spirit. If you need more information, just ask. Spirit will show you the way.

TIPS for the
UNCERTAIN

Have you been asking: "What is next for me?" Your guides want you to make a decision so they can guide you. If you are still unsure, try meditating, be creative and keep the lofty standards you have set for yourself. If you don't make a decision, things will stay the same.

REST

You have been working very hard, and you may be getting tired now, so stop pushing yourself and take some time out to rest.

Try delegating some of your work and dropping some of the responsibilities that have become a burden to you. Your guardian angel will help you to make the necessary life changes.

TAKE TIME OUT

Don't be afraid to spend time alone, because this has many benefits. It clears your mind, improves your creativity, and you will become more focused and more independent.

Being alone slows you down and resets your priorities, so take some time out to explore new possibilities for your life.

AVOID SELF-SACRIFICE

When you try making things better for a lot of people, you may end up making things worse for yourself. A little self-sacrifice is noble, but depriving yourself will leave you depleted. People around you may decide that you don't need anything, because you are the one that's always doing the giving, so you never ask for anything. Take care of yourself, because self-preservation is not selfish – it is essential for living a full and happy life.

BE PATIENT

You may feel that you should be further along the road to development, but you are still in the *gathering* phase, which means you are acquiring new information.

Be patient; when the time is right, you will be called into action.

NOTICE YOUR PROGRESS

Never forget how far you have come and how strong you are. It isn't what you have done in the past that defines you; it's who you are now.

Getting through the traumas of the past has made you the person you are today and the person you are more than capable of being tomorrow.

"Patience leads to power; but eagerness in greed leads to loss."

H. P. BLAVATSKY

CONCLUSION

Spirituality does not come from religion; it comes from the soul, so we should avoid confusing religion and spirituality. Religion is a set of rules, regulations and rituals that have been created by human beings, whereas spirituality is a way of life. It is a network that links us together as one on this planet. I hope this little book gives you an insight into this fascinating subject and helps put your feet on the road to spirituality and happiness.

Good luck.
Tracie